The Young Nigerian Story Book

Story Book

The 26 Stories That Depict The Values Of The Anthem And The Pledge To Nigeria In Relation To The Nigerian Value System

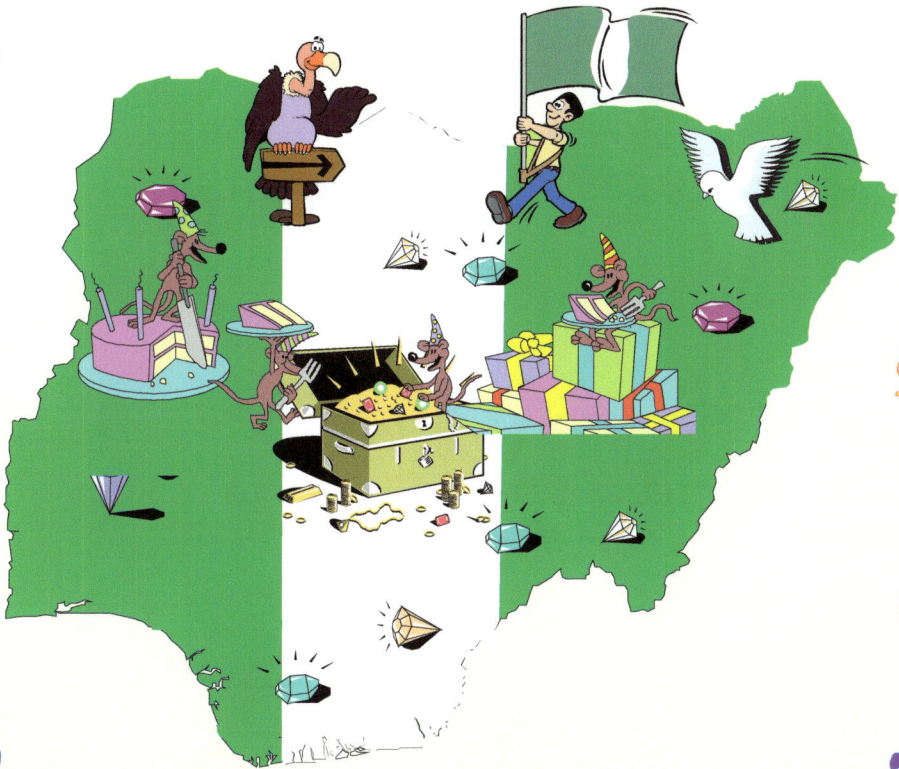

Dipo Toby Alakija

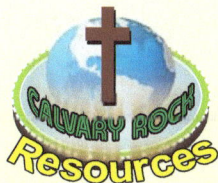

CALVARY ROCK
Resources

ISBN: 978-978-49242-6-9
       978-9784924269

Printed in United States

Published by
CALVARY ROCK PUBLISHING

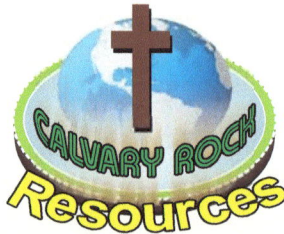

19, Ajina Street, Ikenne Remo,
Ogun State,
Nigeria.

In Conjunction With
CHRISTIAN EDUCATION AND MINISTRATION SERVICES (CEMS)

ACKNOWLEDGMENTS

I must first acknowledge the encouragement we got from various State Ministries Of Education in Nigeria and the Universal Basic Education Board in each State after going through this book and other books titled: "The Values Of The National Anthem And The Pledge To Nigeria," "Building Your Future And The Nation Now" and "Bloodshed In Campus", which is the result of our research works into social vices with particular focus on campus secret cults. All the books, including "The Young Nigerian Story Book" which are approved by these Ministries as subject books in the States are designed to curb the social vices in the society and to be used to build young ones and adults into patriotic citizens of Nigeria. The Federal Ministry Of Education and all the State Ministries Of Education (SMoE) that have encouraged us with the responses are appreciated for their supports.

Secondly, I appreciate the CEMS Project Director, Pastor Samuel A. Ilori who toured round about 30 States in Nigeria to present the books to Commissioners for education and explain the expected results of using the books in the States.

The resource team members of Calvary Rock Publishing And Christian Education And Ministrations Services like Rev. Abayomi O. Solesi, Mrs Omolade Martha Alakija, Pastor Abiodun Adekunle, Evang. Juwon Sokoya, Toluwanimi Margaret Alakija, Lekan Somule, Jonathan Ayeri, Faith Iyanuni Alakija, Juliana Oluwaseun Ekundayo, Blessing Alakija and a host of others are really appreciated.

With the help of God and these people, this book is designed to help Nigerian children to appreciate the meaning of the National Anthem and understand the implication of breaking the pledges they make to the Nation.

With the efforts of our team to package this book, it is our hope that it will influence children who are the leaders of tomorrow to be responsible and valuable in the society.

Dedication

This book is dedicated to all Nigerian parents who are doing all they can to groom their children into reasonable and responsible citizens of Nigeria either within and outside the country.

INTRODUCTION OF THE YOUNG NIGERIAN AND OTHER STORY BOOKS BY THE AUTHOR

It has taken about ten years to package this and two other books titled: Foundation And Young Generation Bible Club Story Books, which are in use in many parts of the world, including US and UK. Thus it will take a while to study each of the three books.

This volume is designed to teach young Nigerians the national anthem and the pledge to Nigeria, impact morals and embed values into their minds through the use of stories and poems.

Studies and personal experience reveal that children are inclined to grow up with what they are made to believe despite genetic, environmental and other factors. Juveniles on the other hand can easily grow out of hand if they do not get the right answers to vital questions about life. Take for instance, a sixteen year old girl who tried to look for reasons she was alive by writing a letter in a book titled "Between Parents and teenagers" by Dr Haim G. Ginott. The letter says, *"the more I read about life's splendour, the more I see its tragedy: The fleetingness of time, the ugliness of age, the certainty of death. The inevitable is always on my mind. Time is my slow executioner. When I see large crowds at a beach, or a ball game, I think to myself: Who among them is going to die first, and who last? How many of them will be dead next year? Five years from now? Ten years from now? I feel like crying out: How can you enjoy life when you know death is around the corner?"*

This youth is at the dangerous stage of life. The answer she gets to a question like this can influence her to turn to God or drugs or any other things that suggest solutions. The contribution or neglect or answers to questions like this when adults were young made them what they are now. The same things are applicable to this girl. All young ones, whether they know it or not, need the help of godly people to guide them in their stages of life. Although, certain genetic factors may influence young ones just like every other human beings, they are not as effective as the education through what they can perceive with their senses in their environment. Invariably, younger generation is the product of the older one through the environment that is created for them. Juvenile delinquency is often as a result of lack of attention of the adults. Parents have put too much of their future into the hands of other people by neglecting their primary responsibilities to their children. The young ones that are left to parent themselves are often the ones that are organized into vice rings. Instead of building more prisons that will accommodate more criminals, efforts should be made by parents; schools; communities; government; private and public organizations to build the young ones in their countries into responsible citizens. The reason is that a neglected child today is the one that turns into a heartless person that gets involved in crimes, posing serious threat to many lives and even the peace of the nation tomorrow. So parents must see their homes and teachers must consider their schools as places where they breed either criminals or responsible citizens of their countries. In essence, a child can be a curse or a blessings, depending on how he or she is raised up. Many potential leaders of tomorrow are being neglected at the time they needed help most. Some adults are bad influence to many young ones. Their conduct and evil communications have corrupted the manners of the young ones.

Young ones at every level need to be disciplined, cultured and tutored about what is expected of them. At that young age, their minds are still very flexible. They are like blank tape that you can record anything you want. Whatever is recorded in their minds is what they would play back to you when they grow older. Although other factors like bad company, ungodly films, television programs and even publications may try to record negative things in their minds but I believe that the positive influence of parents at homes and teachers in their schools can dominate these factors.

This and other books serve the purposes that are indicated in the next page.

In the final analysis, I would like to refer to the old adage that says parents should train their children in the way they want them to go and when they are old, they will not leave the path. Most parents have failed to teach their children family values, leaving them to parent themselves. The result of that is to leave them at the mercy of agents of corruption that now made it possible for a twelve-year old girl to be a mother. Many teachers have also failed in their responsibilities to the nation by failing to teach their students   societal values as embedded in the national anthem and the pledge to Nigeria through their conduct and what they say. Again, the result of that is to have young ones getting involved in vices and even crimes. This book makes attempt to equip teachers and parents with materials that can be used to rebuild the family and the value system of Nigeria through young minds.

- **Dr. Dipo Toby Alakija**

THE PURPOSES AND THE USE OF "THE YOUNG NIGERIAN STORY BOOK" AS SUGGESTED BY THE AUTHOR

It is important to explain the purposes of this book so as to understand how to make best use of it. As indicated in the book titled "The Values Of The National Anthems And The Pledge To Nigeria" which is designed by the author for youths and adults, a close study and comparison of the old, new national anthems and the pledge of Nigeria will reveal the fame work of the Nigerian Value System. This frame work which is neglected is expected to be built upon by everybody in leadership and other positions of influence such as teachers, parents, political and other leaders. The neglect of this frame work is what brings about chaos, vices and crimes in an organized society. Thus "The Young Nigerian Story Book" is designed to teach and embed the values of the National Anthem and The Pledge To Nigeria in relation to the value system through stories and poems. It attempts to interpret the meanings of the anthem and the pledge, boosting their moral values and giving them the picture of what the law says.

The book contains 26 stories, each of which is titled with a line of the National Anthem and The Pledge to Nigeria. The stories are as follow:

THE FIRST STANZA OF THE NATIONAL ANTHEM

THE SECOND STANZA OF THE NATIONAL ANTHEM

THE PLEDGE TO NIGERIA

The book can be studied for more than a session either as a Junior Literary Work materials or Civics or Moral Instruction or other textbooks. This largely depends on the field or skill or creativity of the teacher. As a guide, the followings are the ways the use of the book can be maximized.

ACADEMIC PURPOSE: Since the book introduces civic responsibilities to young minds, it gives them the picture of the Nigerian Value System and makes them to understand that breaking any of the pledges they make to the nation can lead to breaking the law. It also serves as the book that teaches them law, order and the implications of violating them. Apart from this, it recalls a few historical and other facts in the way young minds can comprehend them and appreciate the sacrifices of Nigerian fallen heroes.

LITERARY PURPOSE: The stories and poems are treated in ways that will capture the imaginations of young minds with facts and realities as distinguished from imaginary stories which most children are familiar with. The poems which are to be memorized with the aim of embedding values are also designed to inspire them to be imaginative and creative. Students are encouraged to compose the poems into songs, which can inspire creativity.

PURPOSE OF MORAL INSTRUCTIONS: All the stories are narrated with the aim of teaching one moral lesson or the other. Results of research works reveal that if children are impacted with the belief in God of creation as both the anthem and the pledge indicate, they would be God-fearing as they grow up. God-fearing people are law-abiding people.

OTHER USEFUL PURPOSES: The book can be used to engaged students in extra curricular activities like using the stories they have studied to present dramas, using the poems to compose songs or debating and comparing the activities of characters like mice; menaces and Compatriots in relation to present day events. They can also be made to write their own stories or essays, which may reveal how much they have been impacted.

The students will be impacted if the book is used for these purposes.

STORY ONE

Arise, O Compatriots

Once upon a time in Nigeria, there were many people who were ready to use the gifts like crops, oil, talents and other things which "God Of Creation" gives to the country to bake the cake that would be big enough for both old and young people to eat. When it was baked, it was so big that there were lots of leftovers for children that were not yet born after everybody has taken his or her fair share.

Mice soon found their ways to where good people were baking the cake and began to eat and destroy it. They also destroy the things that were used to bake it. Mice also taught their children how to eat and destroy everything by making them to watch the way they did it. This began to cause lots of problems like shortage of food and money for a very long time. Many people, including children who were once good started looking for food and money by all means. They began to steal and kill one another for money or food. Those who did not want to join them in doing bad things began to suffer so much that they began to die one after the other.

One day someone who was born in the country called Compatriot stood up and cried out to others who were also born in

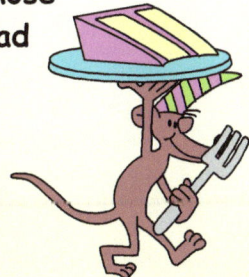

10

Nigeria, "Arise, O Compatriots!" The people stood up at attention as he told them that if they did nothing about the mice that were eating the cake and things that are used to bake it, everybody would soon die of sufferings and hunger.

The Compatriots believed him. They went to get sticks and started chasing the mice away from the cake and the things that are used to bake it. Soon enough, the people began to bake the cake again for the good of both the old and the young ones, including the unborn children.

CAT AND RAT

There is a rat in the room
Sweeping around like broom
Martins hears and sees the rat
It seems so smart and so fat
That he feels it like a loom

He goes out of the room
And calls outside at the cat
Shouting, "chase that cat!"
The cat chase the rat with a zoom
Until it goes into its doom!

Class Activities

1. Teacher: Explain to the students that the cake means the economy. Ask them to list the resources in Nigeria.
2. Ask the students what they can do to stop the mice which represent people who destroy the economy.
3. Ask the students how it would affect them if the mice continue to eat the cake which the people try to bake.
4. Make them memorize the poem about cat and rat.

STORY TWO

Nigeria's Call Obey

There was a time in 1967 when civil war broke out in Nigeria. The Eastern and other States wanted to be a separate county because the Government at that time was not doing what the people expected. Remember the lesson in story one about the mice? This could be one of the reasons the States wanted to break away from Nigeria.

Around this time, a Nigerian soldier who just got married was serving in one of the Western States. His first child who was later called David was born at the time the civil war broke out in Nigeria.

The soldier was rejoicing that he has a son when there was a call that he had to report at the military base. He and other solders were taken to the East to fight the Easterners for trying to break away from Nigeria.

It was a terrible war as citizens killed fellow citizens, causing so many people; including children and their parents to die in the war. When the war started, no one knew when it would end and who was going to die. And so David's father was among those who died in the war. The war made David and so many other Nigerians who were then children fatherless. It also made many women, mostly in the East widows. This affected

their lives.

The call of Nigeria which must be obeyed includes loving one another and putting an end to the killings of people who are created by God of creation!

SOLDIERS AND ENEMIES OF OUR FATHERLAND

Everybody is either a soldier
That fights for our Fatherland
Or the one that fights against it
If you work for the good of others
You are a soldier of our fatherland
If you fight or incite others against it
You are the enemy of our fatherland
We must be soldiers of our fatherland
That care and love others as a family
So that we can defeat enemies within

Class Activities

1. Teacher: Let the students realize the impact of war in the society and make them understand that vices and crimes are also wars.
2. Ask how wars can be prevented.
3. Ask them wrong things people do that make them fight against the fatherland according to the poem.
4. Ask them how it would feel like to lose loved one like a parent. Or how it feels to see a parent crying with sorrow like David's mother.

13

STORY THREE

To Serve Our Fatherland

There was a time in Nigeria when there was wealth which brought good health, prosperity, joy, peace and unity among the people. Suddenly, diseases broke out; making the people sick, poor, sad, troubled and divided. Many people, especially young ones began to die one after the other. You know, if there are no longer children, it would get to a time when the country would no longer exist.

Some Compatriots arouse to obey the call of Nigeria, ready to serve their fatherland by looking for ways to remove the diseases. They found out that one of the main causes of the diseases was rat poison which the people, especially young ones were fond of taking like fruit drinks. The rat poison which always tasted so sweet was actually meant to kill them slowly.

Now Compatriots have lots of problems to solve. First they have to make the people believe that what tasted like fruit drink was actually rat poison. Secondly, they have to start preparing real fruit drinks that would replace the rat poison. Well, preparing the real fruit drinks was not as difficult as making the people believe that the rat poison was not fruit drinks!

This story is actually talking about what is happening in Nigeria. The wealth of the nation are things that give people good health; prosperity; joy; peace and unity; which include

good leadership and stable economy. The diseases are misbehaviours of some citizens, including children and their leaders while the rat poison that tastes like fruit drinks includes bad books, dirty television programs, foul films and music that are entertaining ting but teaching the people wrong things. If people learn wrong things, they will misbehave and become criminals who may be killed or taken to prisons.

RAT POISON

If you really love Nigeria
You will never get the idea
Of giving people rat poison
Which can land them in prison
There are lots of bacteria
That roam around Nigeria
This can lead to crime of treason
Which is a gateway to prison

Class Activities

1. Teacher: Explain to the students in details how things they read, see or hear can make them to be well-mannered or misbehave. Tell them to list and express their views about wrong conduct of people around.
2. Ask them other things that can be considered as rat poison.
3. Tell them to memorize the poem.

STORY FOUR
With Love And Strength And Faith

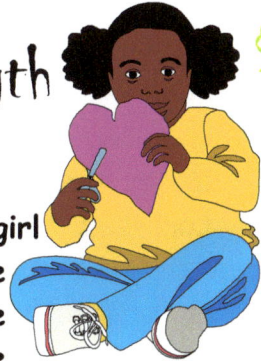

Lara was a Junior Secondary School girl who was well brought up at home. She went to a Primary School where she learnt to behave well. She also to love others through good story books. This made her to be full of strength and faith in God of creation. When she got to Secondary School, most people; including her teachers loved her. She often greeted everybody respectfully and cheerfully. She knew what to say when others were sad. She also loved to share her things with others. Of course, she made friends through her love for others and faith in God, which gave her strength. If you are good to people even some naughty boys and girls would try to be good to you. Although she did not know this, she also has enemies. These include some of her classmates who disliked her so much that they tried to hurt her. Do you know why? If you think it was because they were jealous, you are right. No matter what you do, some people would still dislike you. This is because there are lots of bad mannered people everywhere in the world.

Some naughty boys began to steal and destroy her things like pencil, text and note books where she wrote her notes. When she got home, her mother would scold her. When the teacher asked the students about their note books, Lara would not have anything to show him. The teacher would beat her with cane. When she cried, the naughty boys would laugh. Her friends would feel like crying with

16

her.

Lara prayed to God of creations about the problem until one day the naughty boys had fight among themselves. All of them began to say all the wrong things they have done to Lara, including stealing her books. The matter was reported to the teacher who felt sorry for beating Lara. The naughty boys were beaten with several strokes of the cane.

Some years later, Lara became a medical doctor who has a big hospital while the naughty boys grew into men that begged for money from her.

Class Activities

1. Teacher: Ask the students all the lessons in the story about Lara.
2. Ask them to recite all the titles of story one to four.
3. Tell them to recite all the poems in story one to three

STORY FIVE

The Labour Of Our Heroes' Past

During world war II, it was the custom in the United States for families whose sons were serving in the military to place stars in the front windows of their homes. A gold star, however, means that the son had died in support of his country.

There was a man who was walking down the street of New York City with his 5 year old son at this period. The boy asked his father about the stars at the windows of some houses. His father explained them to him. The boy would clap and cheer each of the families wherever he saw the stars after he was told what they meant. When they came to an empty space which put a gap between the houses, he looked at the sky and caught his breath. There was a star in the sky. He cried excitedly to his father, "look at the star at windows of heaven, daddy! God must have given His Son too!"

The boy was just right because the Bible says in John 3:16, "For God so loved the world, that he gave his only begotten Son, that whosoever believes in him should not perish, but have everlasting life."

When people realize what God has given to them so that they do not go to hell, a place that burns with fire and brimstone, they will use their lives to please him. When they also understand what some Compatriots have sacrificed for the good of the nation during civil war, they will abide by the

18

law and fulfil the pledges they make to Nigeria. If they use their lives to displease God, they make his sacrifice of no value to them and then walk on the path of total destruction. If also Nigerians refuse to fulfil the pledges they make to Nigeria, they make the sacrifices, including the lives of the past heroes useless. The result would be to go into many wars!

SACRIFICE FOR NIGERIA
If you are truly a Compatriot
You will sacrifice for Nigeria
I am a Nigerian Compatriot
I will make sacrifices for Nigeria
By loving other Nigerians
It does not matter where they are
I care for them like my family
Help me to care for them, oh God!

Class Activities

1. Teacher: Using the poem, explain to the students ways they can prove that they love Nigeria and ask them ways they can care for others.
2. Further explain the things that can be considered wars in the society and ask them the lessons in the story about the 5 year old boy.
3. Tell them to memorize the poem.

STORY SIX

Shall Never Be In Vain

A snake went to a chicken that was brooding over its little ones. The snake made lots of hissing sounds and expected the chicken to flee. The snake wanted to grab all the little ones and swallow them as food. The chicken refused to leave its little ones. The snake struck it several times with its venom until the chicken died right on top of its little ones, using its body to protect them.

When it could not get the little ones, the snake went away.

The following day, the owner of the chicken went to the barn to feed it. Through its wounds, he knew a snake must have struck it dead and thought the little ones must be dead too. When he removed the dead chicken, he saw that the little ones were alive and healthy. He was so moved by what the chicken did that he decided that he would not let its sacrifice to be in vain by protecting all its little ones until they grow into big chichen.

All young Nigerians must see themselves as the little ones while the chicken is all the Compatriots who have sacrificed many things, including their lives to protect others from dangers. Snakes are the enemies like kidnappers, ritualists and other evil people

who are ready to kill others for money or power. The owner of the chicken is the Government.

Nigeria is full of snakes that are making life difficult for people. While the Government tries to protect the people from the snakes, the little ones must not let the sacrifice of the Compatriots to be in vain by giving room for the snakes to attack them. They must also do all they can to protect other young ones when they grow up into adults.

NO SACRIFICE, NO HOPE
If there is no one to plant
There would be no harvest
If people make no sacrifices
There would be no blessings
If there is no sacrifices for all
There is no hope for anyone
If all parents make sacrifices
For the good of their children
The nation would be blessed

Class Activities
1. Teacher: Ask the students what they learnt in the story about the chicken and compare it with sacrifices of the fallen heroes during civil war.
2. Tell them to list all the types of people that can be called snakes.
3. Tell them to memorize the poem.
4. Find hard words in story one to six and tell them to get what they mean.

STORY SEVEN

To Serve With Heart And Might

One day, an army general decided to move round the city in his parade van with the best of his soldiers after a major victory over the enemies. This was announced to his soldiers in the city and they got ready for the military parade where the general would pick his choice.

All the soldiers except those who were wounded were present for the parade. They were all smartly dressed, armed with their bogus weapons and other military gadgets.

Just as the show was getting very interesting, a wounded soldier who felt he was the best left the hospital where he was receiving treatments and made his way to the parade ground with a walking stick and blood stained cloths. His head that was full of wounds was bandaged.

The general saw him afar and asked what he was looking for.

He told him he has come to contest as the best soldier. Most of the soldiers laughed at him but when he related what he had to go though in the hands of the enemies while he trying to defend the country, they all knew he had served with all his heart and might. He, therefore, deserved the title of the best soldier in the country. The proofs of his claim as a great soldier were all written in wounds, bloodstained uniform and crutches.

He was made to ride with the general.

The life of a Compatriot is very much like that of the soldier though they are not limited only to the military. Good things you do or give or sacrifice for Nigeria without expecting anything in return makes you one of the best Compatriots.

Dr Ameyo Adadevoh

A Nigerian Physician called Dr Ameyo Adadevoh who was born in 1956 and who died in 2014 was the one that stopped the spread of Ebola virus which could have killed millions of Nigerians. She had detained a Liberian called Patrick Sawyer who was probably sent to spread the virus to kill the people in Nigeria, going by the way he was eager to leave the hospital. Adadevoh died on 19 August 2014 of the disease which she stopped from spreading.

Class Activities

1. Teacher: Tell the students to recall the poems in story 5 and 6. Help them to relate them with what Dr Ameyo Adadevoh had sacrificed.
2. Find out how the story of Ameyo had inspired them to help others.

STORY EIGHT
One Nation Bound In Freedom

Abraham Lincoln was an American lawyer and politicians who was born in 1809. He served as the 16th President of the United States at the period of slavery until he was killed in 1861 for doing the right thing. Civil war broke out during his government, which brought about the end of slavery in American.

Before this time, Abraham Lincoln once watched a plantation owner trying to buy a slave girl whom he suspected was going to be abused.

Lincoln paid the price and set the slave girl free.

After she had been set free, the slave asked him, "does that mean I can say wherever I want to say?"

He replied, "yes."

"I can go wherever I like?" Again he replied, "yes."

With tears running down her face, she said, "then, I'll go with you."

Of course, Abraham took her home and took good care of her instead of using her like a slave. In return, the girl obeyed all his instructions.

Nigerians just like the slave girl were once servants of the Colonial Masters before the independence day in October 1st 1960. After independence day, Nigeria became a free nation. Again, just like the slave girl who subjected her freedom to Abraham Lincoln, Nigerians have to be bound in freedom by the law of the fatherland. This means that just because Nigeria is free from colonial rule does not mean the citizens are free to misbehave. They still have the law which they must obey. Breaking the law can take them to prison, where they would lose their freedom. For this reason, Nigeria is said to be "One Nation Bound In Freedom."

FREEDOM IS A CHOICE
Many people are free by choice
Because they follow the law
Many are in prisons by choice
Because they break the law
Many people will never be free
Because they decide to be slaves
The Slaves of crimes or vices

Class Activities

1. Teacher: Ask the students all they learnt in the story about the slave girl and Abraham Lincoln.
2. Explain the poem. Ask them things people do that take them to prisons.
3. Tell them to memorize the poem or compose it into a song.

STORY NINE
Peace And Unity

There were two young Compatriots called Peace and Unity. They attended the same school in the West even though one of them is from the North while the other is from the East. They have many things in common such as love, faith in God and good behaviours. These made them very good friends. They always ate, played and studied together. There was another boy called Bully who was always trying to cause trouble. Anytime Bully tried to ruin their friendship, they always found a way to come together again.

One day Bully saw Peace mistakenly breaking the ruler which he borrowed from Unity. Bully quickly went to tell Unity that he saw Peace using the ruler to beat the desk until it broke. Unity became so angry that he went to Peace. Without asking him how the ruler broke, he said, 'why do you break my ruler? Next time, I will not give you my ruler!'

Peace was very hurt. He got some money from his mother and went to buy a new ruler for Unity. He gave it him and said, 'you can have this.'

The attitudes of both of them spoilt their friendship. Unity thought it was wrong for Peace to buy another ruler and Peace felt Unity ought not to be so angry at him for mistakenly breaking it. They no longer played with each other as they used to do even though both of they were hurt and lonely without each other's friendship.

During the school fellowship, the Bible Teacher talked about love and read to them

the book of first John chapter 4 verses 7 to 12. Verses 7 and 8. The passage talked about love of God for one another.

   When the boys read the place, Peace went to Unity, taking his Bible and asked. 'Can I sit with you?'

   'Sure, why not?' Unity said quickly. When he sat beside him, Unity asked, "can I read from your Bible while you read mine?' They smiled and exchanged Bibles and read the passage together. They hugged each other and said, 'we'll remain the best of friends which no one can separate.'

I Can Make Good Friends
God gives me my family
And makes for me my country
He gives me power to make things
So I can make good friends
I may make foes that look like friends
Though I will try to make peace with all
Good friends always mean well for me
But foes mean a lot of mischiefs
If I have made foes at any time
God will deliver me from them
Because I desire friends instead of foes

Class Activities

1. Teacher: Ask students the lessons in the story and recall titles in story 1-9.
2. Tell them to memorize the poem.

STORY TEN

Oh God Of Creation

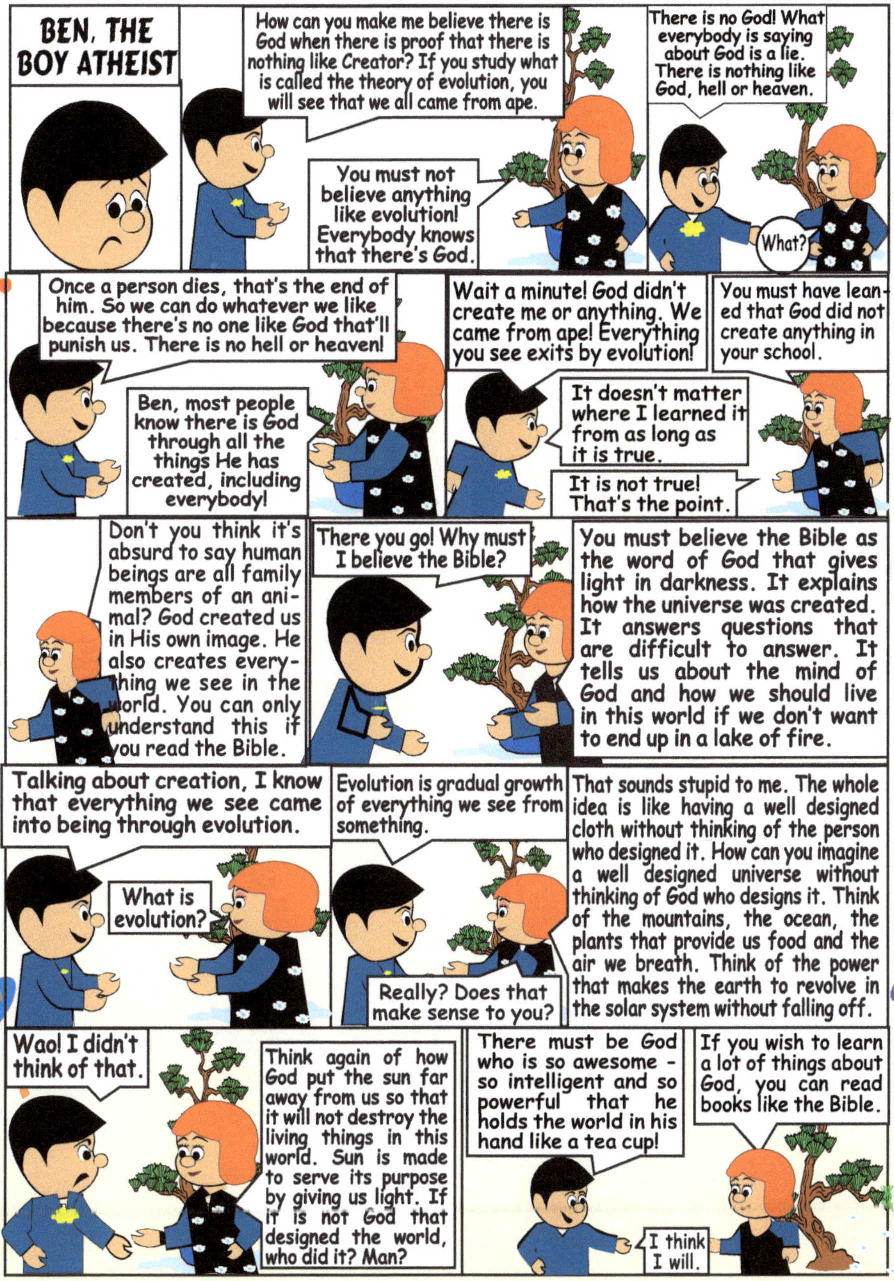

THE GOD OF CREATION

There was a man known as Atheist
He neither believed there is God
Nor believed the world was created
He planted some seeds on his farm
Rain and sun caused them to grow
When it was time for the harvest
Thieves came and took everything
Atheist cried out, "Oh, my God!"

Class Activities

1. Teacher: ask students to list things made by God and ones made by man.
2. Tell them to memorize the poem or make it into a song.

STORY ELEVEN
Direct Our Noble Cause

There is a very beautiful mansion which different groups of people from the same family built. It was built in the way that it can house hundreds of millions of people. There are many precious things in the house, which the people can use to get all the money they need to feed themselves and the children that are not yet born.

One day, the groups of people began to fight over the precious things in the house. All of them think of how to get as many precious things as they can for themselves instead of thinking of how to trade and increase them. While fighting one another, thinking of how to make themselves rich with the precious things, fire suddenly burst out in the house! It begins to destroy many lives and the properties in the house. Children, youths and adults begin to suffer from the fire.

Some Compatriots like Love, Faith, Peace, Unity and others hear the S. O. S (Save Our Souls) call of fellow Compatriots to arise, come together and talk about saving the people and the house from total destruction.

The Compatriots first pray to God of creation, saying to him, "Direct our noble cause," which is to save the people from fire.

Of course, this

story is talking about Nigeria as a big and beautiful mansion. The groups of people who are of the same family are different tribes that are in Nigeria. The precious things in the house are the natural and other resources in Nigeria. The fire is the problems, including crimes like terrorism; kidnapping and ritual killings. The Compatriots are the Nigerian citizens who come together from East, West, North and South to find solution to the problems, asking God to direct their noble cause.

DIRECT OUR WAYS, GOD
Oh, God who created all things
We call on you to save Nigeria
There are SOS calls everywhere
Fire is destroying the people
We are all at your mercy, God!
Teach us to be of help to others
Help us to care for one another
Always direct our noble cause
And guide our leaders right

Class Activities

1. Teacher: Ask of the opinions of the students about problems in Nigeria and ask them how they can put things right when they grow up.
2. Explain to them how the poem is more of a prayer for the nation. Tell them they need to pray for Nigeria.
3. Help them to memorize the poem or compose it into a song.

STORY TWELVE
Guide Our Leaders Right

Note that the title of this story is also part of prayers which young ones must make to the God of creation. Their leaders are people in Governments, school teachers and parents at homes as it would be observed in this story. They must understand that just because adults are doing wrong things does not make them right. They will learn few things in the story which are meant to correct the wrong things which they must have learnt in their environments or through their role models, teachers or parents. The lessons are not about leaders doing the wrong things. It is about young ones learning the right things so that they can grow up to become good leaders in future.

Anita lived in Western part of Nigeria with her parents who were not rich but they could afford to get most of the things they need everyday.

Her mother was fond of borrowing things from the neighbour even though she knew she was supposed to buy those things in the market.

One day, Anita's aunty who was a school teacher in another town came to spend the weekend with them. The few days she spent proved that Anita who was in primary school was learning wrong things through her mother.

On one of the days, the aunty asked Anita whose mother went out on a visit, "where do you keep the matches? I need some in the kitchen."

"There is none in the house, aunty," Anita replied, "but my mother used to borrow

32

some from the neighbours."

"Please, get it for me right away."

Anita went out to get it. She later returned with a full pack of matches.

When she finished using it, she told her to return it. Anita said, "my mother used to take some of it and keep them before I return it. That is what she used to do even if she is given a bottle of oil or a pack of salt."

Her aunty looked surprised and said, "that's stealing!"

"No," Anita said. "Mother does not steal. She told me she takes some of the items in case she needs them next time."

When Anita's mother returned home, the aunty told her she was teaching her little girl how to steal, telling her what happened.

Anita's mother decided to change her attitude for Anita's sake.

Class Activities

1. Teacher: Ask of the students of all the wrong things they see people doing.
2. Further explain the prayer in story 11 in line with the story about Anita and tell them to recite it as a poem or sing it as a song.

STORY THIRTEEN
Help Our Youths The Truth To Know

Now the dove who was brought up with the truth and the vulture who was brought up with lies are two different birds. They have different natures and different characters because they are from different homes. The vulture was made free to do whatever he liked and to eat anything that tasted like food to him, including rotten meat.

The dove was made to know and say the truth, always doing what was right at home. He was also trained to eat only what was good for him.

The vulture who wanted to change dove to his ways of life made friends with him. They would have made good friends if they were not from different places. This made them different from each other.

'I can teach you how to eat rotten,' said the vulture.

The dove made faces. "We don't eat rotten meat where I come from. My parents said it may kill me if I eat anything like that."

'Don't be a mama's pet! Everybody eats it. Come on, let's go over there and try it,' the vulture said. 'I've eaten it many times. It is delicious.'

The dove picked the rotten meat and tried to eat it. It smelt horrible! How was he supposed to eat a thing like that? It would trouble his stomach.

'Come on, eat it up,' the vulture persuaded him. 'Watch me...' He picked part of the meat and ate it. 'Yummy! I love it. Come on, try it...'

The dove tried again. Making faces, he put it in his mouth... hmmm... raw, rotten meat! Disgusting! He thought, 'oh, I must not make the vulture feel disappointed.' He swallowed it. 'Ooh, terrible taste!'

'Delicious, isn't it?' asks the vulture.

The dove said, 'it is good.' But it was not good for his stomach because the meat would not digest. It was kept rotten inside his stomach. It caused him much pains until he died few days later.

This story is about a child who is well brought up at home and in the school. He is taught the truth that if he behaves well, he would live long but if he joins bad gang which is the vulture that always makes others to do wrong things like stealing and fighting, he may die young. The bad gang makes the good child to become bad. As he grows up, the wrong things he has learnt make him to break the law until he is killed or taken to prison.

Class Activities

1. Teacher: Ask the students what they learnt in the story about the dove.
2. Further explain the poem in story 9 in line with the story above and tell them to compose the poem into a song.

STORY FOURTEEN
In Love And Honesty To Grow

Once upon a time, some Compatriots from East, West, North and South called Faith in God Of Creation, Love Of Fellow Citizens, Peace Of God, Unity Of The Nation, Strength Of The People and others went on a biking competition. The first person to complete the race would get a gold medal, the second would get silver while the third would get bronze.

Before that day, the Compatriots have prepared very hard so as to make the region they represented proud. Of course, the citizens in all each region were watching the competition, praying to the God of creation to make their region to take the gold or silver or bronze medal.

As soon as they were commanded to take off, all the Compatriots began the race. The crowd that was watching them through network of televisions began to cheer the people. Love was taking the lead, followed by Faith, Unity, Peace and the rest. Suddenly, the handle of Peace' bicycle loosened and twisted. He lost control of the bicycle and had an accident. He cried out with pains as his body was dragged on the road.

When the rest heard his cries, they were disturbed. Love who was still taking the lead was the first to stop because he knew he must not leave his brother and friend behind and go after the gold as the crowd expected.

The rest of the Compatriots cried at him, 'why do you stop the race?'

Love replied, 'my brother is more important to me than the gold. You can go ahead and get the gold. I am going to help my brother.'

The rest of the Compatriots were moved by Love's action. They also stopped the race and went to help their brother on his feet. They all knew that he would have done the same for them if they were in his shoe. No one won the official gold or silver or bronze because no one completed the race but they all won the hearts of the crowd who gave them much more gold.

IN LOVE AND HONESTY
He who loves people loves God
He who loves God will be honest
A honest person is progressive
He who thinks more about gold
Instead of the good of others
Can become enemy of others
The enemies of the citizens
Are enemies of the nation
That can lose their freedom

Class Activities

1. Teacher: First relate the story about the compatriots with people that cause problems because of money and ask them what they learned.
2. Interpret the poem about love and honesty as part of the major means to move the nation forward.
3. Help them to memorize the poem or compose it into a song.

STORY FIFTEEN
And Living Just And True

John was being taught to live a just and true life at home and in the school but he chose to be stubborn and unruly until the day his mother made some spaghetti for the family to have as dinner. She had also fried some chicken and kept it in the fridge for the next day. John who hated to eat spaghetti said, 'mum, I want rice and fried chicken.'

His mother told him to go to bed hungry if he did not want spaghetti.

Angrily, John went to bed but he could not sleep because he felt hungry.

After everybody has gone to bed, he sneaked into the kitchen to take part of the fried chicken in the fridge.

He sat beside the fridge in the dark, eating the chicken in the kitchen.

When his mother heard noises in the kitchen, she went to the place to find out what was there. She asked in a low voice, 'who is there?'

Of course, John kept silent. He thought she would soon go away. When she did not go, he grunted and made noise like a wild animal.

His mother ran back out of the place and went to call his father who was sleeping. She woke him up and said, 'there is a wild animal in the kitchen!'

His father quickly stood up from the bed and went to the place.

John heard their footsteps as he was still enjoying the stolen chicken. He made another wild noises though he was still chewing the meat.

His mother ran again but his father did not. He took a long stick of a mob that was closed to him and walked quietly to the side of the fridge where the noise came from. Because it was too dark to see, he did not know it was John sitting down, eating his mother's chicken. He struck him on the head.

John fell down on the ground, opening his mouth as if he was dead. The chicken fell out of his mouth.

His father said to his mother, 'I've killed the animal bring the light.'

When she brought the light, they discovered that it was John. He was unconscious. Looking surprised to see him, they took him into the room.

John who was wounded later woke up with heavy bandage on his head.

It was then he knew the reason he must live a just and true life, which means always doing the right thing all the time. He dared not steal again.

Class Activities

1. Teacher: Recall the poem in story 8, titled freedom is a choice and relate it with the story. Ask students the ways of living a just and true life.
2. Ask them other ways of living unjust and untrue life.

STORY SIXTEEN
Great Lofty Heights Attain

Richard was the smallest boy in the class though he was not the youngest. His parents were so poor that they could hardly give him and their other children everything they need. This made him looked so weak and small.

All other students normally laughed at him. They would call him names like "Richard, the small boy" or "Richard, the weak boy." He could not play football like other boys. He could not answer any of the questions the teacher asked him in the class even if he knew the answer. He was always afraid that the rest would laugh at him if he tried to do anything. His mates maltreated him in the class. He thought he was not a normal child.

One day, his mother took him to a birthday party where he met many other children. Because he was made to feel bad about himself, he went to sit alone somewhere. A boy called Moses went to make friends with him. Soon they began to talk about many things. Richard told Moses how the students in the class treated him.

'If they treat you like that,' Moses said, 'you don't have to feel bad about yourself. You must believe what the God of creation says about you. God of creation says you're beautifully and wonderfully made. You can still reach great and lofty height in life where other students would respect you. You can begin now by doing some good things which they cannot do.'

Richard became excited about what he learnt from his new friend. From that day, he began to study hard. He also practiced how to run fast. When his mother sent him on an errand, he would run there as fast as he could. Guess what was the result of the study and the practice. He came third in the examination. During the school inter-house sport, he got a gold medal in relay race! Then many children in the class began to make friends with him, calling him new names: Richard, the brilliant boy or the medalist.

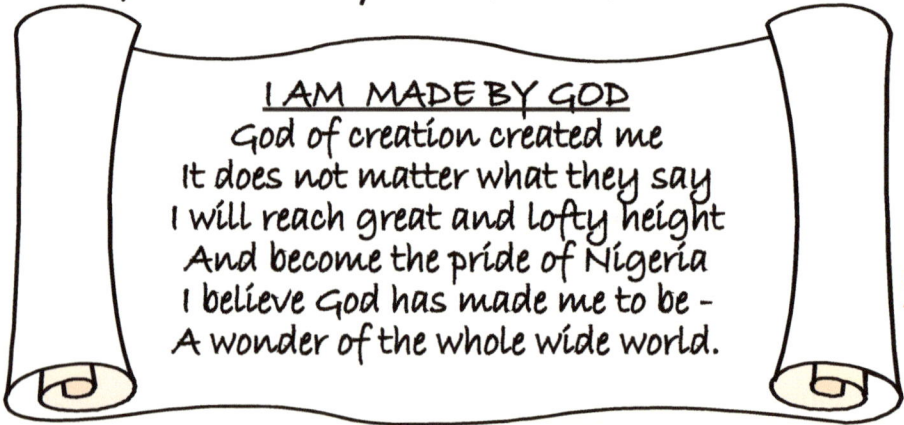

I AM MADE BY GOD
God of creation created me
It does not matter what they say
I will reach great and lofty height
And become the pride of Nigeria
I believe God has made me to be -
A wonder of the whole wide world.

Class Activities

1. Teacher: Ask what the students learnt in the story above and point it to them that everybody has a gift.
2. Ask them how they can use their gifts to reach great and lofty height.
3. Tell them to memorize the poem.

STORY SEVENTEEN
To Build the Nation Where Peace

The sea was once calm and peaceful as all fishes and their little ones went about their activities. Both old and young fishes were free to move up and down until some sharks invaded the sea, killing so many fishes for food.

There was a Mother Fish whose husband was killed by one of the sharks when going to look for food for the family. This gave Mother Fish the burden to look after their three little ones Called Disobedience who was born first. Curious was the second while Obedience was the last child.

The little fishes lived in a small house called Safe Haven with their mother who always tried to protect them from sharks.

She always prayed to God of creation to help and protect them as she went around the sea that was full of sharks for food and other things they would need in Safe Haven. Although she warned the little ones of the danger outside Safe Haven, Curious asked her one day, 'why do we have to stay in Safe Haven?' Mother Fish told them that when they grew older, they would understand. She could not tell them about the sharks because she thought they might be so afraid to live in the sea that they would run to another place where they could die easily.

Disobedience felt she was old enough to find out what was

happening outside Safe Haven. She decided to go out to look for fun with other young fishes who also believed they were old enough to be on their own. As they were having fun, a young shark who pretended to be one of their friends told them to follow him to a funfair where they would enjoy themselves. When they got there, other sharks captured and ate them up as food.

Later, Mother Fish told the rest of her little ones more about the sharks. They never disobeyed their mother until they grew up enough to find a way to drive the sharks out so that peace may reign in the sea again.

LET PEACE REIGN, OH GOD!
God of creation we call on you
Let there be peace in our country
Make us to fear you in our ways
So that we can be all law-abiding
Use us to put wrong things right
So that we can enjoy your peace.

Class Activities

1. Teacher: Explain the sharks as those who threatens the peace of Nigeria, ask and suggest how to stop them.
2. Ask or explain to them how God-fearing people can abide by the law.
3. Tell them to memorize the prayer.

STORY EIGHTEEN
And Justice Shall Reign

There was a king called Justice who used the staff of office called Truth to rule in Niger Area called Nigeria. The name of Nigeria was coined from the two words by Flora Lugard, wife of Fedrick Lugard who was then Governor General of Northern and Southern Protectorates.

Since Justice reigned with the use of Truth, which always revealed secrets of mice to him, he was able to get Compatriots like Obedience, Love, Strengths, Honesty, Faith, Peace, Unity and others to rule with him.

A mouse called Deception wanted to rule Niger Area so as to eat up the cake, which the people have laboured to bake since Justice had been on the throne. He planned with other mice like Dishonesty, Lies, Fraud and others to steal Truth from the Palace in the place called Aso Rock. When they were able to steal the staff, they removed Justice with the cabinet of Compatriots from office and began to rule over Niger Area.

The people soon began to suffer from much pains, sorrows, hunger, horror and even loss of lives during the reign of Deception. Everybody started crying for Justice to come back and reign but he was nowhere to be found. They went to the few Compatriots around and told them to do something about the mice, saying, "if you don't bring Justice back to the throne, mice will kill everyone of us; including our children."

44

The Compatriots knew they were right. So they gathered in one place and prayed to the God of creation to direct their noble cause.

The compatriots and the people later began to search for Justice.

They found him alone in a place called Neglected while his cabinet members were found in a place called Rejected.

All the Compatriots led the people to Aso Rock and take the staff of office from mice. Then they put Justice back on the throne as the king.

WHEN TRUTH IS MISSING
Wherever truth is missing
Justice can never reign
When Justice does not reign
Criminals become the leaders
Whenever a criminal is a leader
Crimes are the order of the day
Crimes are enemies of the people

Class Activities

1. Teacher: Explain the meaning of the story for the students to further comprehend and ask them what they have learned from it.
2. Tell them to recall all the titles in story 1-18, using it to sing the anthem.
3. Tell them to memorize the poem.

STORY NINETEEN
I Pledge To Nigeria, My Country

There were some children who were born in different parts of Niger Area called Nigeria. They attended different private and Government schools but they were all made to make the same pledges to their fatherland, saying, "I pledge to Nigeria, my country."

The God of creation who was their witness as they made these pledges decided to bless anyone that fulfill his or her promises and punish anyone that dared to break them.

As time went by, some of these children began to grow into Compatriots like Obedience, Love, Strengths, Honesty, Faith, Peace and Unity who would become leaders in different walks of life as in law, management, civil service, engineering, medicines, education, politics, security and others.

Many other children began to grow into menaces like Lies, Examination Malpractice, Deceptions, Dishonesty and Frauds that give births to vices that cause people to suffer or crimes that make others to lose their lives.

As years rolled by, the young compatriots grew into great leaders like honest business people that help others who are in need, good lawyers who helped to get poor but innocent people out of legal problems, responsible political leaders, reasonable teachers who impacted good knowledge into others and other successful and wonderful people that make Nigeria great.

The young menaces also grew into mice that grieved their fatherland when they did not fulfil their pledges. Because of this, God of creation began to punish them for the wrongs or crimes they have committed. Some of them were infected with diseases that caused them to suffer. Some were killed while fighting the police while some went to prisons where they cannot see their loved ones or get married or raise children.

While Compatriots were full of joy and blessings of God who rewarded them for fulfilling their pledges, mice were full of pains and sorrows.

THE PLEDGE TO NIGERIA
The pledge to Nigeria is good for us
Because it makes us very successful
The pledge to Nigeria is better for us
Because it makes us very responsible
The pledge to Nigeria is best for us
Because it makes us wonderful people

Class Activities

1. Teacher: Explain to the students how breaking the pledges to Nigeria is breaking the law. Ask them what they learn in the story.
2. Explain how the pledge can make them wonderful as in the poem.
3. Tell them to memorize the poem.

STORY TWENTY
To Be Faithful

There were some menaces called Unfaithful, Undesirable, Unwanted and others among the soldiers who felt they should rule Nigeria by force. So they decided to remove the rulers through what is called Coup d'etat. They have tried many times to overthrow the Government. Some of the attempts failed while some were successful. Each time they succeeded, some people; including Compatriots like Faithful, Loyal, Honest, Patriotism and Courage would die trying to stop them. If they failed, all menaces that were involved would be killed. So in any case, Coup d'etat is often a time of danger for Compatriots among the soldiers who need to prove their love and faithfulness to their fatherland by fighting the menaces. It is also a time for the menaces to die if they fail in their efforts to overthrow the Government. Coup d'etat is often a game of deaths, a deadly weapon of terrorism and panic.

There was a time again when the people were to elect their leaders through what is called Democratic Process or Election after those who wanted to be in Government have persuaded the citizens to vote for them.

After the election, the menaces in the military struck and took over the Government. Through out the years they ruled, the people suffered pains, sorrows and poverty. The

48

menaces did not care about the people at all. So they cried to God of creation to save their fatherland from the menaces.

God of creation heard their prayers and struck the leader dead on the bed. Some Compatriots took over the Government and use Democratic Process to allow the citizens who is eighteen year old and above to elect the Government of the people, by the people and for the people. This type of Government is called Democracy.

THE PLEDGE TO BE FAITHFUL

To be faithful to God
Is to love one another
Because we are his people
To be faithful to Nigeria
Is to make peace with others
Because we are all Nigerians
To be faithful to our fatherland
We must care for one another
And stop the violence in the land

Class Activities

1. Teacher: Find hard words in the story above and explain them to the students and further explain the effects if there is violence in Nigeria.
2. Ask students of their views about the people that are considered menaces. Teach them of the need to pray for them to change instead of feeling bad.
3. Tell them to memorize the poem.

STORY TWENTY-ONE
Loyal

There were two girls called Loyal and Faith. Though each came from the Western and Southern parts of Niger Area, they went to the same school in the North where they were taught about love of their fatherland by loving one another, no matter where they come from.

Faith grew up into a full time housewife of a very rich man from the East known as Chief while Loyal became a lawyer, living with her husband and children in the North. Though they were far away from each other, they remained friends until Chief was poisoned by a menace in his family who wanted to take over his properties. The poison later killed him. This made Faith and her young children very sad. As they were crying over the dead, the menace went about telling other members of the family that it was Faith who killed her husband so that she could inherit the properties.

The family believed the menace and sent Faith and her children out of the house. When Loyal heard what happened, she left her own family in the North and went to the East to fight for her friend and sister.

They prayed together to God of creation to help them fight the menace.

Loyal began to find out how and who poisoned Chief while at the same time she went to court to argue that the family has no right to sit over Chief's properties. She argued that Faith and her children owned them.

Later the menace who poisoned chief was discovered through the housemaid. She said she saw him putting the poison in his drinks.

The menace was later handed over to the police and the properties were given back to Faith.

Faith wanted to give Loyal lots of money but she refused it, saying, "I didn't do it for money. I did it because you are my sister and friend. I also did it so that 'justice shall reign' as we have it in the national anthem."

After defeating the menace, Faith with her children took Loyal who had become their heroine to the airport where she took off to the North.

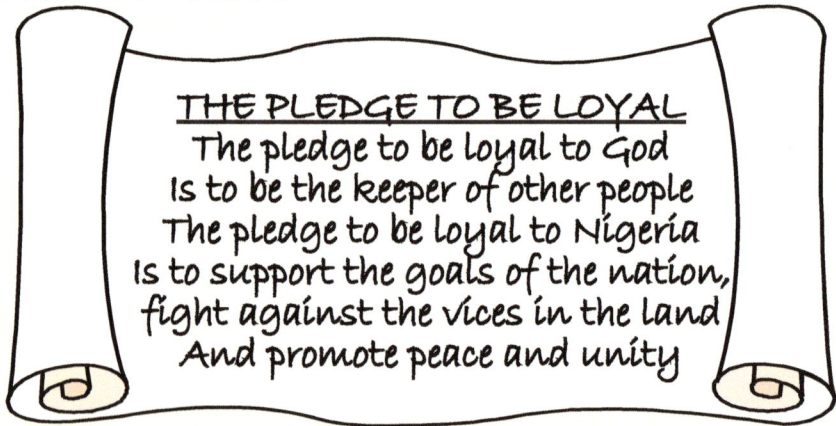

THE PLEDGE TO BE LOYAL
The pledge to be loyal to God
Is to be the keeper of other people
The pledge to be loyal to Nigeria
Is to support the goals of the nation,
fight against the vices in the land
And promote peace and unity

Class Activities

1. Teacher: Ask the students what they learnt in the story.
2. Let them know that through love and care for one and another, they can overcome menaces.
3. Tell them to memorize the poem.

STORY TWENTY-TWO
And Honest

There were two boys called Honest and Dishonest who went to the same school. They were always taught to be well behaved. The teachers told them during Moral Instructions class that if they wanted to be great and successful in life, they must study their books and fulfill all the pledges they made to Nigeria, which is their fatherland.

Honest tried to study his books and fulfill the pledges but he could not understand many things that were taught in the class. So he failed during the examinations. Dishonest did not read his book at all but he managed to pass because he cheated during the examination. He was promoted to the next class while Honest was made to repeat.

Honest cried and said to himself, "I should have cheated too so that I can get promoted like Dishonest" but the teacher that gave them moral instructions encouraged him. He said, "if you don't repeat the class, you will not know what you are supposed to know before you move to the next class. If you study your books well, you will pass and get promoted. The reason you come to school is to learn, not just to pass the examinations."

Honest was encouraged. He studied and worked hard to get promoted and become successful while Dishonest continued to cheat during the examinations.

Some years later, Honest graduated from the

University and became a Lawyer. He later became a Judge while Dishonest who never stopped cheating grew into menace called 419. He always looked for quick and easy ways to make lots of money.

One day, the police arrested Dishonest for using tricks to steal money from a company. He was charged before the court. Do you know who the Judge was? You are right if you say it was Honest.

Honest judged and sentenced Dishonest to prison according to what the law says even though they were once classmates.

THE PLEDGE TO BE HONEST
The pledge to be honest to God
Is to be truthful in everything
The pledge to be honest to Nigeria
Is to deal with others in truth,
Instead of taking short-cuts
That can cut people's lives short

Class Activities
1. Teacher: Ask the students what they learned in the story.
2. Ask them of their opinions about the Judge who sentenced his classmate to prison.
3. Tell them to memorize the poem.

STORY TWENTY-THREE
To Serve Nigeria With All My Strength

There were four young Compatriots who came from the Eastern, Western, Northern and Southern parts of Nigeria. They all wanted to serve their fatherland with all their strengths in a noble cause of nation building. This noble cause includes going from one place to another, teaching the people about building the nation through the use of their talents and strengths.

One of the Compatriots called Lame did not have legs to walk but he has the brain to plan how to build the nation. Another one called Blind could not see but he knew how to talk to people and make them build the nation. Another one called Dumb could not talk with his mouth but he has very strong body. Another one called Stone Deaf could not hear at all but he has sharp eyes that could see when danger was coming to the Compatriots.

Lame began to plan how they would start moving. He told Dumb to carry him on the shoulder and told Blind who was going to talk with the people to hold one of Dumb's hands. He made Deaf to lead them and watch out for danger that might want to stop them in their noble cause of building their fatherland. Whenever they came across any menace, the Compatriots would combine their strengths and fight him until they defeated him.

With time, they were able to get to the people. Blind was made to talk with them about Lame's plan on how to build the nation. He was able to persuade them to join the group. Before long, everybody except the mice and menaces began to build the nation; including baking the national cake.

This story talks about the people in Nigeria. Each person has gifts that may be different from that of others. A person who is not so brilliant may be gifted in sports that can bring pride to Nigeria. Another person who is not be good in science subjects which can make him a doctor or engineer or nurse may be good in art subjects that can make him a teacher or writer or lawyer or other experts. Others who are not able to get higher education can become good business people or industrialists or other experts.

What is important to note in the story is that if you use your gifts for the good of other people, God of creation will bless you through them.

TO SERVE WITH STRENGTH
To serve God with all my strength
Is to give my heart to God of creation
To serve Nigeria with all strength
Is to serve the people with my gifts

Class Activities

1. Teacher: Ask of the students to recall the titles in story 19 to 23.
2. Ask them what they gain in the story and memorize the poem.

STORY TWENTY-FOUR
To Defend Her Unity

There is a tug of war going on in Niger Area between Compatriots and menaces who have teamed up with mice. The Compatriots are doing all they can to defend the unity of the nation through what they say and do while the menaces are trying to tear the nation into shreds through many ways. Menaces are dividing the citizens by telling them to cause trouble which can lead to the kind of civil war that broke out in 1967.

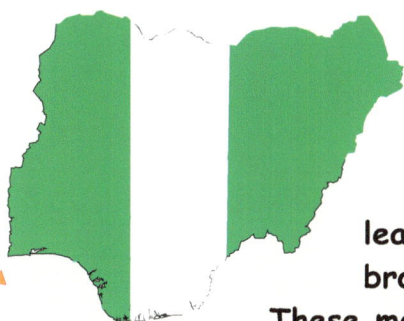

These menaces and mice who seem to be increasing as they get citizens to join them believe that if they can divide the country, they can take the rich part and rule the area. They do not know that the behaviours of citizens are the real riches of the nation. What that means is that if the nation has nothing like oil, gases and other things but has Compatriots that are ready to build the nation with their talents and gifts, it would become rich, peaceful and successful. On the other hand, if the country is rich with oil, gasses and other things that can bring money but the fatherland is filled with mice and menaces like the ones in Nigeria, they would destroy these things and make the people to suffer hunger in midst of plenty food.

Because Compatriots believe in God of creation who wants everybody to live in peace and joy, God is on their side. He gives them the strengths to fight the mice and menaces who are causing trouble, pains and sorrow.

With God on the side of Compatriots, more citizens; including children join them in the fight to reduce menaces and mice. Since they have made pledges to their fatherland, they continue the fight until mice and menaces are locked up in prisons or removed from Niger Area.

TO DEFEND THE UNITY OF NIGERIA
I must defend the unity of Nigeria
By promoting peace and harmony
I must defend the unity of Nigeria
By showing love to fellow Nigerians
I must defend the unity of Nigeria
By campaigning against menaces
So that mice and vice will disappear

Class Activities

1. Teacher: Review all the stories about menaces and mice and tell the students to compare their natures with Compatriots'.
2. Ask them the reasons they need God to fight mice and menaces.
3. Tell them to memorize the poem.

STORY TWENTY-FIVE

Uphold Her Honour And Glory

Once upon a time in Niger Area, it was a shame to be called a citizen of the country. Most other countries believed everybody was a rogue because there were so many mice and menaces within and outside Nigeria. These mice and menaces were fond of using tricks to take money from people. So the Governments of other countries warned their citizens who wanted to do businesses with Nigerians to be very careful.

The author wanted one of his books to be published by a publishing company in United States. The publishers told him to prove it that he was really the author since there were many rogues in Nigeria back then.

The author who had pledged to Nigeria when he was in school that he would "uphold her honour and glory" said to the publishers, "I can only prove it to you that there are more rogues in your country than in my country." Then he decided to become a publisher in his country and continues to "uphold her honour and glory" even though there were so many menaces that bring dishonour and shame to Nigeria.

You too can make a difference from the mice and menaces in the society by doing the right thing every time and by doing the followings:

1. Study and work hard to be part of those who will uphold the honour and glory of Nigeria. It is a shame to cheat during

examination.

2. Stay away from vultures who can teach you to eat "rotten meat" if you cannot change them from menaces to Compatriots.

3. Always practice all the good things you can do best so that you can be the best or be among the best in the world.

4. As the next story is going to teach you, believe in God of creation who will never allow menaces to harm you or your future. When you believe in God, you will become a God-fearing person who is law-abiding. If you are God-fearing, God will order your steps and make you great.

TO UPHOLD HONOUR AND GLORY

To uphold honour and glory of Nigeria
I will never cheat during examination
To uphold honour and glory of Nigeria
I will not eat rotten meat of the vultures
To uphold honour and glory of Nigeria
I will fight against menaces and mice
God will help me for I am a Compatriot!

Class Activities

1. Teacher: Ask the students what they learned in the story.
2. Tell them to recall the 4 things they must do to make difference from menace and list things that can bring shame to Nigeria.
3. Tell them to memorize the poem.

STORY TWENTY-SIX
So Help Me God.

There were twin sisters who lived with their aged grandmother. Granny as she was called by the twin sisters strongly believed in God of Creation. She took care of them and taught them about faith and trust in God. They have a farmland where they planted crops for sale or for food. God always brought them great harvest in the farm by giving them rain. Because she knew it was God that provided for them, Grammy also taught the twin sisters of the need to share their things with needy people.

There was a time when rain did not fall. This caused famine in the land. Because of this, there was lack of food and money to buy all they needed.

The twin sisters and Granny felt the famine so much that they always prayed that God should continue to feed them.

One day, Granny felt like eating some bread but there was no money to buy it. The twin sisters and Granny decided to pray about it in the sitting room, saying, "Oh, God of creation, you have always provided for us. Please, give us some loaves of bread and some butter."

Some naughty boys who did not believe there is God heard them praying. They said among themselves, "let us give them some bread and butter. It will make them feel it is God who gives them. When they finish eating, we will go and tell them we gave them and not God because there is no God."

"That is a brilliant idea. It will make feel like fools for believing in God."

They contributed some money and went to buy loaves of

60

bread and a thin of butter. They threw them inside the sitting room through the window.

The twins and Granny were happy when they saw them. They thanked God for the food and ate some of the bread and butter, keeping the rest.

As they finished eating, the boys came into the house to tell them they were the ones that gave them the loaves of bread and butter, not God.

One of the sisters argued, "It is God who gave us when we prayed."

"We threw the bread and butter inside when we heard your prayers."

Granny said, "God gave them to us even if he sent little devils to give us."

The boys were disappointed when they heard that. They hoped to make their faith in God appeared foolish. Now Old Granny made them appeared like the foolish devils that God used to give them bread and butter!

TO UPHOLD HONOUR AND GLORY
To uphold honour and glory of Nigeria
I will never cheat during examination
To uphold honour and glory of Nigeria
I will not eat rotten meat of the vultures
To uphold honour and glory of Nigeria
I will fight against menaces and mice
God will help me for I am a Compatriot!

Class Activities

1. Teacher: Ask the students what they learnt in the story.
2. Review titles of all the stories
3. Make them sing the anthem and recite the pledge.